1/09

AR PTS: 0.5

Tower of London

England's Ghostly Castle

By Gail Blasser Riley

Consultant: Stephen F. Brown, Director
Institute of Medieval Philosophy and Theology, Boston College

BEARPORT
PUBLISHING

New York, New York

Credits

Cover and title page, © ACE STOCK LIMITED / Alamy; pages 4–5, © Adam Woolfitt/ CORBIS; 6, © The Art Archive; 7, © Taxi Collection/Getty Images; 8, © London Aerial Photo Library/CORBIS; 10, © www.britainonview.com; 11, © Hamburger Kunsthalle, Hamburg, Germany/The Bridgeman Art Library; 12, © Society of Antiquaries, London, UK/The Bridgeman Art Library; 13, © Erich Lessing/Art Resource, NY; 14, © Erich Lessing/Art Resource, NY; 15, © Jonathan Blair/CORBIS; 16A, © The Granger Collection, New York; 16B, © National Portrait Gallery of Ireland, Dublin, Ireland/The Bridgeman Art Library; 17, © www.britainonview.com; 18, © Harrogate Museums and Art Gallery, North Yorkshire, UK/The Bridgeman Art Library; 19, © The Granger Collection, New York; 20A, © Tim Graham/CORBIS; 20B, © TIM GRAHAM/Alamy; 20C, © TIM GRAHAM/Alamy; 21, © Private Collection/The Bridgeman Art Library; 22, © Fine Art Photographic Library/CORBIS; 23, © Mary Evans Picture Library/Alamy; 24A, © Jonathan Blair/CORBIS; 24B, © Jonathan Blair/CORBIS; 25, © Catherine Karnow/CORBIS; 26–27, Graham White; 29, © www.britainonview.com.

Publisher: Kenn Goin
Project Editor: Adam Siegel
Creative Director: Spencer Brinker
Original Design: Dawn Beard Creative and Triesta Hall of Blu-Design

Library of Congress Cataloging-in-Publication Data

Riley, Gail Blasser.
  Tower of London : England's ghostly castle / by Gail Blasser Riley.
    p. cm.
  Includes bibliographical references and index.
  ISBN-13: 978-1-59716-249-4 (lib. bdg.)
  ISBN-10: 1-59716-249-3 (lib. bdg.)
  ISBN-13: 978-1-59716-277-7 (pbk.)
  ISBN-10: 1-59716-277-9 (pbk.)
  1. Tower of London (London, England)—Juvenile literature. 2. London (England)—Buildings, structures, etc.—Juvenile literature. 3. Great Britain—History—Juvenile literature. I. Title.

  DA687.T7R55 2007
  942.1'2—dc22

                2006012276

For more information, write to Bearport Publishing Company, Inc., 101 Fifth Avenue, Suite 6R, New York, New York 10003. Printed in the United States of America.

10 9 8 7 6 5 4 3 2 1

Table of Contents

A Ghostly Past

For hundreds of years, people heard footsteps when no other humans were near. They saw ghostly figures floating down the hallways. Some ghosts carried their heads. Some had no heads at all.

In 1817, a guard and his family sat down to eat inside the Tower of London. In horror, they saw a ghostly bottle floating in midair. A light-blue liquid bubbled inside. As the bottle neared the guard's wife, she screamed. "It has **seized** me!" The mysterious object then floated away.

Many reports of ghostly figures in the Tower had come before this one. Many more were yet to come.

Some people believe that the Tower of London is the most haunted building in England.

The Tower Begins

In 1066, an angry William of Normandy sailed across the English Channel. King Edward had promised William that he would be the next king of England. Yet just before King Edward died, he passed the crown to his brother-in-law, Harold Godwinson.

William was determined to be England's next ruler, however. He and his army sailed from France to England. They fought and **defeated** King Harold.

William (right) is shown killing King Harold (left) at the Battle of Hastings.

After defeating King Harold, William became known as William the **Conqueror.**

As the new king of England, William built many wooden **forts** to protect his land. Around 1078, William ordered one of his wooden forts to be torn down. He replaced it with a strong stone **fortress**. It was to become the first part of the Tower of London.

The stone tower King William built is the oldest part of the Tower of London. At 90 feet (27 m) high, it was the tallest building in London at the time.

A Safe Tower

The Tower of London was never meant to be the main home for England's kings and queens. Instead, rulers often used it as a safe place to live during dangerous times. Part of the Tower was also used as a prison to hold enemies.

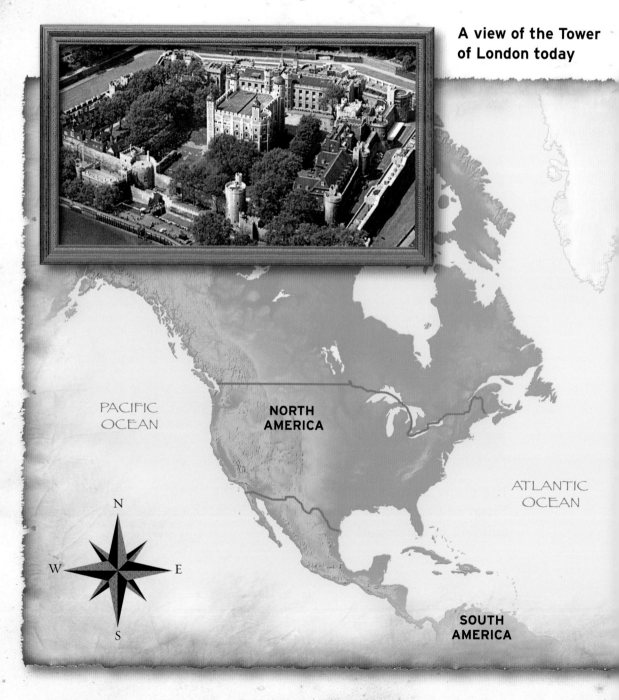

A view of the Tower of London today

PACIFIC
OCEAN

NORTH
AMERICA

ATLANTIC
OCEAN

N

W   E

S

SOUTH
AMERICA

By 1220, Henry the Third was king of England. He knew it was important for a ruler to have a strong fortress. To protect his castle, King Henry built a stone wall around it. A **moat** was added outside the castle walls.

King Henry also **whitewashed** King William's original stone tower. The building was now called the White Tower.

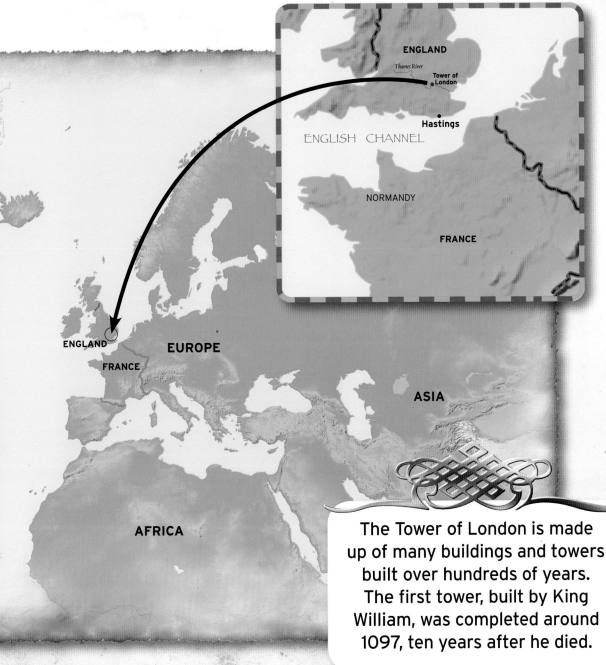

The Tower of London is made up of many buildings and towers built over hundreds of years. The first tower, built by King William, was completed around 1097, ten years after he died.

The First Ghost

The walls that King Henry the Third built around the Tower of London didn't just protect his castle. They were also the scene of the first ghost sighting there.

Traitors' Gate

Henry the Third's son, Edward the First, added a water gate to the Tower. It was later called **Traitors'** Gate. Prisoners in a boat would pass through this entrance on their way to the prison inside the Tower.

Legend has it that a ghost appeared one evening while the castle walls were being built. He seemed unhappy that the walls were being added. So he struck one of them. The wall collapsed into a pile of rubble.

Who was this powerful ghost? Many people believe that it was **Archbishop** Thomas Becket. Henry the Third's grandfather had caused his death in 1170. Now Becket's ghost was making trouble more than 50 years later.

Archbishop Thomas Becket being murdered

Princely Ghosts

From 1455 to 1485, two different royal families fought for the right to rule England. Edward the Fifth was the rightful **heir** to the throne. Yet he was only 12 years old. So in 1483, Edward and his nine-year-old brother were moved to the Tower of London for safety. They were placed in the Garden Tower. During this time, the children's uncle, Richard the Third, was crowned king.

Richard the Third

The princes were never seen again. Many people believe that Richard ordered his nephews to be killed so that he could become king. After the boys' disappearance, the Garden Tower became known as the Bloody Tower.

A painting of the princes locked in the Tower

For centuries, people claimed to see the princes' ghosts, hand in hand, floating down staircases in the Bloody Tower.

The Headless Wanderer

In 1533, King Henry the Eighth married Anne Boleyn. He hoped that they would have a son who could rule after him.

Queen Anne did have a child, but it was a daughter, Elizabeth. King Henry began to lose interest in his wife. He wanted to marry another woman who would give him a son. So in 1536, Henry **imprisoned** Queen Anne in the Tower. About two weeks later she was **beheaded** on Tower Green.

A painting of Anne Boleyn (kneeling) after she was arrested and imprisoned in the Tower. Some say that Anne Boleyn is the most famous ghost who haunts the Tower.

Since Queen Anne's death, people have often reported seeing her ghost—without a head. They watch Anne lead other ghosts to the spot where she was buried. Sometimes, people say, she carries her head as she wanders.

Tower Green

Tower Green was an open piece of land inside the Tower where people were beheaded. Anne Boleyn's ghost is often seen there.

A Prisoner for Many Years

Anne Boleyn's daughter, Elizabeth, eventually became queen of England. She ruled from 1558 to 1603. The queen was fond of a sailor and explorer named Sir Walter Raleigh. Yet he married another woman. When Queen Elizabeth found out, she had him imprisoned in Brick Tower for five weeks.

Queen Elizabeth the First

Sir Walter Raleigh

After Elizabeth died, her cousin became King James the First of England. In 1603, he ordered Raleigh back to prison for trying to plot against him. He was placed in the Bloody Tower, where he remained until 1616. Upon King James's order, Raleigh was beheaded in 1618. Ever since, tales have been told of his ghost wandering around the Tower.

One of Sir Walter Raleigh's rooms in the Bloody Tower

Raleigh lived comfortably in the Bloody Tower with his family and servants. He had many visitors while in prison.

The Gunpowder Plot

King James the First was not liked by his **subjects** because of religious disagreements. In 1605, a group of people planned to blow up the king and other government officials. Guy Fawkes, an English soldier, was in charge of setting off the **explosives**. He hid in a cellar below the building where the king would appear. However, he was caught before he had a chance to use the gunpowder.

Guy Fawkes being brought before King James the First

Fawkes was imprisoned in a tiny **cell** in the Tower. He was tortured until he confessed his crime. On January 31, 1606, he was hanged. Ever since, people have claimed to hear his painful screams echo through the Tower.

Guy Fawkes about to be hanged

Fawkes's prison cell was so small that he couldn't lie down or stand up straight in it.

A Royal Theft

King Charles the Second ruled England from 1660 to 1685. During that time, one of the Tower's most popular attractions—the Crown Jewels—was first displayed. The Crown Jewels were safely locked up in a cage made of strong iron bars. Or so it seemed.

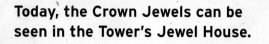

Today, the Crown Jewels can be seen in the Tower's Jewel House.

In 1671, an Irishman named Thomas Blood became friends with the jewel guard. Blood convinced the guard to show the royal treasures to him and a few friends. When they met by the jewels, Blood threw a cape over the guard's head. Another man smashed his head with a **mallet**. Blood stole the royal crown and ran. Yet he was soon caught.

Thomas Blood and friends trying to escape after stealing the crown

Although Blood was captured, he was soon **pardoned** by King Charles the Second. No one is quite sure why.

Animals in the Tower

People were able to visit the Tower as early as 1660. By the 1800s, the Tower had become a popular tourist spot. People liked to visit the Royal **Menagerie**. Animals, including lions, tigers, eagles, and porcupines, were kept there. Yet, did other animals lurk at the Tower?

Visitors getting a tour of the Tower in the 1800s

One night around 1815, a guard turned to see a huge ghostly bear in a doorway. The guard attacked the terrifying animal. Yet his weapon passed right through the bear. In fright, the guard passed out. Two days later he died.

The Tower's Menagerie grew so large that in the 1830s the animals were moved to the London Zoo, shown here.

The Royal Menagerie was a collection of animals that was kept in the Tower. It probably began in 1235 when Henry the Third received a wedding gift of three leopards.

The Yeoman Warders

The **Yeoman Warders** began working for King Henry the Seventh around 1485. Their job was to keep the king safe and to guard prisoners.

The Yeoman Warders and their families live within the Tower of London.

A Yeoman during the Ceremony of the Keys

For about 700 years, the Tower of London has been locked up every night during the Ceremony of the Keys. The Yeoman Warders perform this seven-minute ceremony at 9:53 p.m.

Today, Yeoman Warders still serve at the Tower. While there are no longer prisoners to guard, Yeoman Warders are an important part of many Tower ceremonies. They also give tours and care for the ravens that live around the Tower's grounds.

Hundreds of years ago, ravens arrived at the Tower of London. A legend grew that if the ravens left, the Tower and the country of England would fall. So the Yeoman Warders have made sure that the ravens never leave.

The ravens' wings are clipped so that they can't fly away from the Tower.

Visiting the Tower of London

Today, the Tower of London is one of the most famous tourist attractions in the world. About 2.2 million people visit each year.

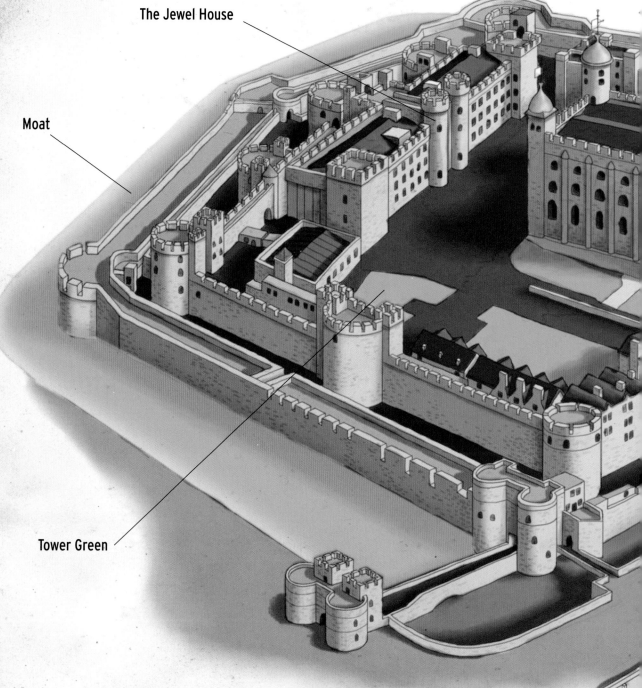

The Jewel House

Moat

Tower Green

The Yeoman Warders offer guided tours of the Tower and its grounds throughout the day. They discuss the history of each spot with visitors. Wandering through the castle's towers and buildings, tourists can relive nearly 1,000 years of England's royal—and ghostly—history.

The White Tower

The Bloody Tower

River Thames

Traitors' Gate

The Tower of London is surrounded by a moat on three sides and by the River Thames (TEMZ) on the fourth side. Today, the moat is dry.

Just the Facts

♧ Only seven people were beheaded within the walls of the Tower of London. The beheadings all took place on Tower Green. Many other prisoners were killed in public on Tower Hill.

♧ Beginning in the 1200s, coins were made in the Tower of London. Money continued to be made there until 1812.

♧ On August 15, 1941, World War II spy Josef Jakobs became the last person to be executed at the Tower.

♧ The Crown Jewels are still worn by England's royal family to special events. When the jewels are temporarily removed from the Tower, visitors may see a small sign that says "IN USE" in place of an item.

♧ Many of the buildings in the Tower of London were used as storehouses for military supplies. In 1670, more than 10,000 barrels of gunpowder were stored there.

Timeline

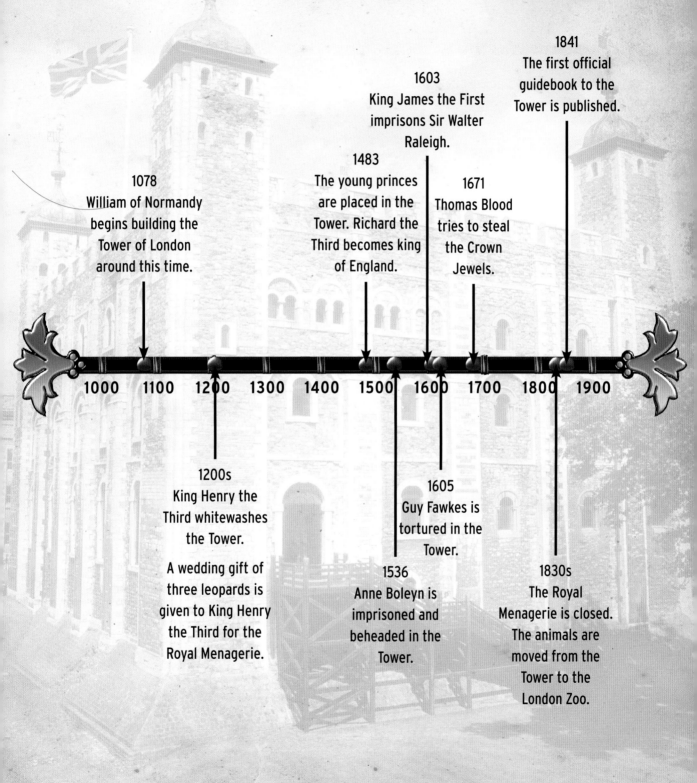

1078
William of Normandy begins building the Tower of London around this time.

1200s
King Henry the Third whitewashes the Tower.

A wedding gift of three leopards is given to King Henry the Third for the Royal Menagerie.

1483
The young princes are placed in the Tower. Richard the Third becomes king of England.

1536
Anne Boleyn is imprisoned and beheaded in the Tower.

1603
King James the First imprisons Sir Walter Raleigh.

1605
Guy Fawkes is tortured in the Tower.

1671
Thomas Blood tries to steal the Crown Jewels.

1830s
The Royal Menagerie is closed. The animals are moved from the Tower to the London Zoo.

1841
The first official guidebook to the Tower is published.

1000 1100 1200 1300 1400 1500 1600 1700 1800 1900

Glossary

archbishop (*arch*-BISH-uhp) a high-ranking bishop who supervises other bishops

beheaded (bi-HED-id) had one's head chopped off

cell (SEL) a room in a prison

conqueror (KONG-kur-ur) one who defeats someone else

defeated (di-FEET-id) beat someone

explosives (ek-SPLOH-sivz) substances that can blow up things

fortress (FOR-triss) a strong building from which people can defend an area

forts (FORTS) buildings that are made to withstand attacks

heir (AIR) a person who will receive money, property, or a title such as "king" or "queen"

imprisoned (im-PRIZ-uhnd) locked up

legend (LEJ-uhnd) a story that has been passed down from years ago

mallet (MAL-it) a hammer

menagerie (meh-NAH-juh-ree) a collection of wild animals

moat (MOHT) a wide ditch dug around a palace or castle that is filled with water

pardoned (PARD-uhnd) excused or forgiven

seized (SEEZD) grabbed hold of

subjects (SUHB-jikts) people who are ruled by a king or queen

traitors (TRAY-tuhrz) people who have betrayed others

warders (WORD-urz) prison guards

whitewashed (WITE-*wosht*) painted white

yeoman (YOH-muhn) a servant in a royal household

Bibliography

Diehl, Daniel, and Mark P. Donnelly. *Tales from the Tower of London.* Gloucestershire, England: Sutton Publishing Ltd (2004).

Hahn, Daniel. *The Tower Menagerie: The Amazing 600-Year History of the Royal Collection of Wild and Ferocious Beasts Kept at the Tower of London.* New York: Penguin (2004).

Hibbert, Christopher. *Tower of London.* New York: Newsweek Book Division (1971).

Lapper, Ivan, and Geoffrey Parnell. *The Tower of London: A 2000-Year History.* New York: Osprey Publishing (2000).

Wilson, Derek. *The Tower: A History of the Tower of London from 1078 to the Present.* New York: Encore Editions (1979).

http://tudorhistory.org/castles/tower/

http://whc.unesco.org/en/list/488

Read More

Cohen, Daniel. *The World's Most Famous Ghosts.* New York: Aladdin (1989).

Fisher, Leonard Everett. *The Tower of London.* New York: Macmillan (1987).

Hynson, Colin. *The Tower of London.* Milwaukee, WI: World Almanac Library (2005).

Learn More Online

Visit these Web sites to learn more about the Tower of London:

www.historicroyalpalaces.org/webcode/tower_home.asp

www.nationalgeographic.com/ngkids/0101/tower/

Index

About the Author

Gail Blasser Riley is the author of dozens of books for children and adults.
Her books have received honors from the Children's Book Council,
the New York Public Library, and Young Adult Library Services Association.